Reincarnation & Other Stimulants:

Life, Death, &
In-Between Poems

Reincarnation & Other Stimulants:

Life, Death, &
In-Between Poems

By

Ken Craft

Cover design by Lauren Craft

ISBN: 978-1-954353-74-9

Kelsay Books
502 South 1040 East, A-119
American Fork, Utah, 84003

Thanks to my wife, Jill, for her constant support and love. Much appreciation to my daughter, Lauren, for her creative help with both the cover and the website, kencraftauthor.com. As for my son, Jeff, who wonders when the novel will arrive, I can only say, "Keep the faith!" Much appreciation and love to my parents, my brothers, and their families. Finally, to loved ones who have gone before me, you are still writing my poetry.

Acknowledgments

Grateful acknowledgment goes to editors of the following journals, where the following poems first appeared, sometimes in slightly different versions:

Aethlon: Journal of Sports Literature: "A Boy and His Basketball"
American Journal of Poetry: "My Old School"
Chronogram: "Act V"
Connecticut River Review: "Mystery"
DASH Literary Journal: "To a Depressed Friend"
Deep Wild Journal: "Thoreau Knows"
Funicular Magazine: "Self-Diagnosis"
Gray's Sporting Journal: "Maine Deer Hunt"
The High Window (UK): "Synchronicity"
The MacGuffin: "The Poetry of Naps," "To Be"
Maine Sunday Telegram: "Core Body Temperature"
Miracle Monocle: "A Boy, A City," "Loyalty"
Misfit Magazine: "Skipping the Funeral Reception"
Offcourse: "False Spring," "First-Person Solipsist, "Old Dog
    Poem"
One: "My Brother's Bedroom"
Orchards Poetry Journal: "The Duck Blind"
Pedestal Magazine: "The Phoebe Nest"
Pidgeonholes: "How the Dead Speak"
Plainsongs: "Thoreau Reconsiders"
Red Eft Review: "A Death Next Door"
Sheila-Na-Gig online: "Meditation Lesson," "Rosa Raises Red
    Flags," "Territories"
South Florida Poetry Journal: "Crazy Cat Lady," "The Morning
    After"
Tipton Poetry Journal: "Rip"
Typehouse Magazine: "The Farmer in Time"
Westchester Review: "Death of a Conversation"

Contents

OLD BEGINNINGS, NEW BEGINNINGS

MY BROTHER, MY SELF

My Brother, My Self

Your brothers, they're all alive, aren't they?
Who is this dead brother, anyway? What does he look like?

What does he look like? He looks like I once did.
Only stupid and naïve. Which is what cost him in the end.
You know what the world does with stupid and naïve.

Actually, I don't. Care to explain? We have time.

They separate from people who age. From bodies that cling to
long lives for 30 pieces of silver. But not him. He mastered change.
He stayed a beautiful kid, one I never appreciated
        until it was too late.

Now he's the snow globe shaken by memory's hand,
snowing forever because he can.

*

YOUNG & OLD

"The root of suffering is attachment."
—Gautama Buddha

Synchronicity

Maybe because the deep freeze
was almost Biblical in duration.
Maybe because it's early March
and 55 degrees. Most likely it's that
nurturing sun-sky without clouds
(unless you count six softly expanding
contrails slowly stitching white on blue).
It feeds the itch to move because movement
is life, which must mean it's a sign
that a little girl on the opposite sidewalk,
a short-leashed box kite bouncing
behind her, is running and laughing
alongside her Golden Retriever
at the exact moment this breeze
brings a burst of pine needle
to the nose, and I hear icicles drip
black-water bull's eyes into puddles
below the eaves of a neighbor's house,
reminding me of public fountains in the cities
of my youth—water wobbly with
copper wishes and silver dreams.
Which must explain why I'm being eyed
by a snowbank's crevice, its shadowy cave
a pocket of inhaled blue. This as that Boeing 737
up there and that chainsaw shredding air
somewhere fuse like the last circling ouroboros.
Some song self-consuming, I think, lazy
yet satisfied. A sleepy sound reminding
me of childhood, of thoughtless happiness,
of that brother lost in a frigid fissure
of the brain. The brother left decades ago
at a January bus stop, where innocence

piled up in drifts, where no caves of blue
preyed upon once-upon-a-days like this,
ones crowned by a nurturing sun-sky without
clouds (unless you count six softly expanding
contrails slowly stitching white on blue).

One Sunrise

A psychologist once told me insomnia
Is a sign of depression, which is why
I'm leaving the house early so I can find
A field still smoke-drunk in its hollow of fog.
There I'll lie on my back, thinking of her,
Waiting for the sun—round russet resolving sky—
To cotton through an eastern wood softly.
A chef once assured me alcohol dissipates
In a sauté pan, leaving only flavor as memory.
Today I feel like simmered wine seasoning
Its repast of remorse as the sun heats to new coinage
And mist thins to tenses past and imperfect, leaving me,
Drowsy and parched, a lone bay leaf begging to be
Scraped from the bottom of this scorched-pot life.

My Brother's Bedroom

Mother steps past the worn bedroom rug
and a kept bed, sheets crisp beneath,
bedspread fenced in brown and black
plaid. The tiny lamp on a nightstand remains,
its yellowed shade smiling with cowboys
waist-deep in lasso circles, pistols and holsters.
From the window, she can spy the sagging
swing set, bent beam alive with the thrum
of a nest, rusty holes inhaling dark whispers
of wasps as they return from where they came
in the endless cycle of being. Morning after
morning, my mother translated by glass,
the room a black veil behind her as she counts
the prodigal returns of each sleeping sting.

Skipping the Funeral Reception

Just for Tom, I drive to my childhood neighborhood, streets
shrunk by the decades, pausing by the mouth of the Masons'
garage where Cal's Yamaha "Fizzie" felt its first hunger,
where his father's MG rested on wood blocks blackened
by gasoline, oil stains, and sullenness. Cal, the first to die
in a heap of bike and red maple resistance, his life now
a weathered cross-stick in the knapweed off River Road.

The widow Seavey's house is next door, its paint curling
like birch bark. Her porch, airy and empty, was once home
to a wrought iron table topped by a cookie jar filled with
hermits—brown sugar and molasses, their warmth soft
and sweet with summer afternoons.

Then Merilee Miller's bone-colored split ranch. The girl
who belittled tough boys like us when we wore eye black
for football, calling it a hidden urge for make-up. A suicide
in her forties, someone at Tom's funeral told me.

And the hill we tobogganed after snow, a crouching,
embarrassed knoll between houses that harbor hidden
interlopers speaking names only I can hear: Seavey,
Mason, Miller. The board and batten of memory.

Cal, Merilee, my brother. And me, just from the funeral
of the fourth—Tom. The boy we shoved because we could.
Chiclet smile. Blue eyes of hero worship. Stopping
on the corner, looking at the saltbox Cape, I can see his mother
lifting the window sash, calling after her son, her voice fighting
wind out of the north: "Tom, you going caroling with the boys?"

Yes. Tom with the rest of us just this once. Heading up the hill
under a lead-box sky one brazenly-cold Christmas Eve Day.

Boys so happy and sure we even let Tom tag along.
"Joy to the World" rising in brief breath clouds.
Mouths filled with the lie of immortal life.

A Death Next Door

My neighbor died last week.
The plastic-wrapped newspapers,

Yellow, blue, unread,
Congregate at the end of her driveway.

The tongue of the mailbox
A communion of catalogues and bills,

Postcards to the dead.
I call the post office, recycle old news,

Wait for a strange car, sudden moving truck,
Distant relative, but none appear.

Each day, before dawn, the street flows dark
Below the grassy banks of her house.

Its candlelight bulbs illuminate all but one
Window, as if Advent were April, as if spring

Were prying open a final window,
Trying to ignite its square of trapped night.

The Body Occupied

A lifetime's experience
with pain
teaches us
that it always
departs if you're patient,
measures taken
or not.

Time is the great
healer, after all,
just like the ocean
my grandmother
took me to swim in
if I had a cut
or infection.

See how the cold salt
soothes? she said
of the puffy wet
white curling
round the red wound.

See how God creates,
then provides
for his children until
the end of days?

Or, as she forgot to add,
until pain comes
like a squatter
waiting in your kitchen,
Smith & Wesson
in its lap.

Loyalty

Darkness changes everything
on a dock, especially when the lake breaks
in ripple-speak like sleep against riprap
behind me. Ears and eyes adjust
to the sound of water, to the slide of clouds
that let only rare, fugitive stars out and, briefly,
the red ember of Mars being breathed on
by the past so that it flares warlike,
so that the dead—who once called this island
home—can return like Odysseus
in disguise to the loyal dog that is me.

A Boy, A City

That boy followed by the hound? He's the King of Dogs
& indolence, crowned by the heat, smelling of sweat & summer,

Finely brushed by the down of roadway dust. His soles
Are gentle maps—finely cracked rivers of earth.

He wears his sovereignty in his walk. Old & middle-aged men,
Fat & napkin-bibbed behind restaurant glass as they swallow their

Foie gras & sip their Sauternes, forget that one can own
Without being owned. To them & others along these streets,

He is just another boy with nothing. Small matter to someone
Who sees the world for what it is & must be because, truth is,

His eyes, all hazel & hasty movement, hold keys to the city's
Sun-seized walls, its oak doors buckled in bronze handles,

Its stone ramparts, gates, & columns, always ready for review.
What others ignore, he lifts from the dirt & cups in the warmth of

His curiosity. Stale bread heel? He shares its crust with the dog.
Coin smoothed by the years? He slides it into the lip of his pocket.

The thinning one thinking about a hole. When he is
Tired, the shaded cool of a granite bench shelters his sleep

From the soft heaviness of afternoons. When he is thirsty,
The sound of water—jeweled rush jetting richly into the

Fountain's rippling smiles—calls his name. There you will
Find him, this lifetime & next, forever boy slaking his

Forever thirst, cooling the brown reed of his body—restive,
Regal, still reckless with the sweet beguilement of youth.

Mystery

They were simply sounds of summer:
       the faraway buzz of a chainsaw,

the drawn-out drone of an airplane,
       the stridulation of crickets in fields of wildflowers.

Somewhere a block or more away, the bark of dogs
       and the fading wheels of trucks as rubber

memorized highway from New England to Florida.
       Voices close enough to hear, far enough to misunderstand.

High winds swaying white pines, maples, beeches.
       How it sounded like surf looking for its ocean.

Someone's lawnmower, a woodpecker rapping a rotting tree
       and, during gray days, rain on macadam, a metal roof,

downspouts and bluestones at their base. The mystery?
       When summer sounds became lonely ones.

A Boy and His Basketball

Turning on Elm, I braked
for a boy dribbling his basketball
in the street before a crooked hoop
that had been winged by a winter plow.

His open coat spoke of March winds,
and his knit Celtics hat dreamed off the curb
like a green and white cat in its warm curl of sunlight.

Hearing my car, he hurried a last-second three,
catching only breeze and bird song,
then stood inside what would be the key,
hands on hips, breathing the hours,
not bothering to look and see who or what
rolled over the pothole near center court.

I liked that about him.
And how my rearview mirror
showed him resuming his game,
attacking the rim with higher percentage shots,
this time dribbling behind his back
for an imaginary crowd,
scoring layup after layup
against the porous defense
of his loneliness.

Warring Angels

Every angel is terrifying.
          —Rilke

My brother and I laughed
when Father Kelly said bad angels

hovered over the streets of Hartford
like killer bees homing on vice.

But I've lived long enough to sense how celestial
strangers can lay siege to the imagination:

columns of smoke and fear, dust devils
touching down on the thinning years.

It's one guardian angel vs. all those fallen ones,
underfed and ornery, craving the blood of pasts

still rich with regret. So, forgive me,
Father, for I have sinned yet again.

Today I turned and caught death
at his own trick—off guard. Instead of angels,

though, death as unfinished fresco of rain,
pine limbs, and windblown leaves.

As green-slurried life. As grackle tails inhaled
by the burning heads of October's fiery trees.

Core Body Temperature

You, the former waterskiing champion of Maine,
wanting, one last time, to immerse yourself in the lake
on this 90-degree day in the arms of a son
who struggles under the weight of your bloated body.
Your skin frogs across the cradle of the boy's biceps
as he fights gravity and sweat, walks robotically,
releases you in three feet of water so you can kneel
in muck. You move your eyes behind sunglasses
as if searching for lost years hidden in the shoreline's shade.
Soon you're in teaching form again, explaining the science
of lowering core body temperatures, how it happens
when you submerge in cool water long enough,
how it's an old Army trick borrowed from an old Indian one.
Remember that, you tell your son, as the soft marl
of the lake bottom shifts, rising from under your knees,
beginning to trust them.

The Morning After

The kitchen ceiling is a soft cirrus of cigarette smoke,
and the white globe light Mom loves glows like a full
gaseous moon. Below, a table of highball glasses, cards,
coin kitties, napkin-bedded baskets, chips and Chex mix,

ashtrays of butts bent 90 degrees, some ringed with lipstick,
some slipped off the edge. Sounds tinny and thin through
the tube of time: radio jazz, Kennedy halves, quarters
sliding like silver pucks across polished wood. In memory,

hours and minutes sprint by, stopping only for Sundays. Talk
and laughter grow louder as we grow little-kid groggier, falling
asleep in our beds up the hall, dreaming of family, friends, and
neighbors who never grow old and never feel pain and never die

of lung cancer or cirrhosis of the liver or, God save us, natural
causes. In memory, we eat Trix or Cocoa Puffs or Frosted Flakes
as Mom comes out of her room in a housecoat Sunday morning.
She's squinting against a sunrise of empties and glasses half-filled

with dead ice, the accordioned remains in ashtrays, the wounded
bottles of liquor, brown and green and clear. She's turning back
for the refuge of her room, saying: "Boys, could you put the bottles
away for me, please? I can't stand looking at them in the morning."

Father & Son

We sit out on the patio, my dad and I.
He's sweating under the open sky
Of that overcast word, octogenarian.

He talks about bluebirds, how strange
That they are eating the suet this year.
Aren't they supposed to eat flying insects?

And the Carolina wrens, how they have not returned
To the ceramic birdhouse he affixed
Beneath the gutter three years ago.

Book propped against it, my New England stomach
Bulges toad-belly white in the morning sun.
"Watch you don't burn," Dad warns distractedly

Before moving on to the weather—the little rain
They've had, the approaching dog days and the chances
Of another drought. "If only we could wring

The humidity here," he says. "Like wet towels,
Always weighing us down. Snowbirds come here
For this heat. Believe that? To hide in the AC."

He gets quiet, and the wind kicks up,
Blowing flaps on the table umbrella shading him.
His eyes take a contemplative glaze. A mockingbird

Sings somewhere high in the beech tree. I hear a slap
As Dad swats a mosquito. The muscle below his upper
Arm briefly swings like a half-filled water balloon.

"Look at this," he tells me, holding his arm aloft.
Small wrinkles intersect the skin from every direction
Like a fine mesh net lifting fish heavy with lost fight.

"Damn old-man skin," he says, addressing his own arm
As if it's some solicitor coming to interrupt—our
Conversation, the South Carolina heat, everything.

Death of a Conversation

Peter catches me between front door and car,
pretends to weed around marigolds. "Oh, hey."
That casual greeting his specialty. Daily conversations
mostly desultory before he breaks into his pet topic:

suicide. I know, a bad sign, but idle talk of killing himself
is Pete's sole joy in life. At least he's not overly repetitive.
He's too much the reflective lapsed Jesuit for that.
"That blinding light they talk about at the end," he says.
"All bullshit. Black as coal dropped down a well at midnight,
if you want the truth. You recall anything—
a blessed thing—before you were born?"

I want to say yes, I do, in fact. Make up stuff
about bullets bubbling the surf off Normandy,
the stench of canvas and sleeping soldiers in tents
under Shiloh's heat, the wet patch of earth stuck to
Squanto's umber knees as he finally stands
in his Pilgrim field of corn seed and fish corpse.

"It's what makes death so easy," he says. "It's why
every fool manages it so professionally. It's not
like we meet some snowy-bearded Maker
after unmaking ourselves—an angry God
directing us to Hell for jay-walking violations."

Mercifully, he never talks ways and means. Never razors
or hoses from exhaust pipes to windows of opportunity.
And certainly never the taste of metal, the last bullet
train to nighttime Tokyo.

"In fact, it'll be peaceful, like the Garden of Eden
before the damn fruit and the sweet-talking serpent. Trust me."
I want to trust him. I do. But I have to buy a quart of 2% milk.
A dozen pastured, cage-free eggs. Unbleached flour.

"Deer been at your hydrangeas again," I note, pointing.
He glances at his patch of Eden, and I take the opportunity
to tell him I have to go. We all do, eventually.

Territories

Prisoner of time, white-
suited transient gone to
Territories of his own making,
Twain sleeps *in medias res.*

Huck, however, lives on.
Slipped free of plots
and conflict, caught between
boy and manhood, wandering
where innocence wavers
like an August horizon.

Hanging off the raft, his feet
point like pale rudders, river-
rinsed, ten toes compassed west.
Downriver he'll land and light out
for Territories once more, trusting
instinct and wariness to shield
him from drunken schemers
and grifters slick as catfish.

See the blue tendrils of pipe
smoke floating into lazy sky?
The ones sniffing out freedom
and falling stars? That's Huck,
all right. All the unwritten parts.

Crazy Cat Lady

A friendly neighbor told me first. Crazy Cat Lady, who lived on the hill across the street, died Monday night. I did not know her, but I knew her garbage. Instead of using receptacles, she drove down her long driveway to deposit plastic bags of trash. On cue Wednesday mornings, congregationalist crows tore them open, lobbing litter like dogs digging showers of dirt: used Kleenex, Amazon-dot-cardboard, crusty Lean Cuisine trays. But especially cat food tins reeking of salmon, chicken, and Cat Lady indifference.

Tired of picking up wind- and crow-blown refuse, I took to tossing cat food tins back on her driveway each night. Listening to the tinkling sound gave me Old Testament pleasure. The euphony of light landings on macadam! That and hearing the wheels of her Ford flattening Fancy Feast cans into coins of retribution.

And though her death gave me pause, I'd be less than honest if I didn't acknowledge the ancillary succor. No more marching around my lawn plucking cans by flashlight! No more flinging diminutive tin Frisbees across the street!

Only later did I consider her cats. How they might be meowing in dark rooms every night. Rubbing against empty Cat Lady cardigans hanging from Cat Lady chairs, the cotton still smelling of Cat Lady cologne. Pressing paws against cool windowpanes while staring hungrily across the street at the farmer down below. The man who once harvested cans of cat food by flashlight.

Hidden Oracles

Heat is the only drug that works. The old man
lies in his bath of Epsom salt, play-drowning
the persistence of pain in his body, tracing

memory to the happy amnesia of fifteen and, for fifty
minutes, listening to the fat drip of the years fall
from the faucet. He emerges a stranger—skin

raw and ruddy—towels off, shuffles to the hall floor.
Here it's one knee at a time, then two palms flat, before
slowly turning to press his bony back against wood's

honest coolness. His heart, jumping for breaths,
pumps too fast. His chest rises and falls. His eyes
scan shells and fans in the white paint above.

He hasn't read ceilings since he was a kid finding
dragons or witches, giants or trolls scattering men
and women with bulging eyes and screaming mouths.

The faces no longer frighten him. Here's one that's kind as
Cassandra with her milky rills of hair, starlit eyes, mouth
fraught by words so foreign they dam against the ear.

Another looks like that boy chased by the wolf, its tongue
dripping saliva and sincerity. The boy's expression is clear.
His lips extend into the lupine letter "w": "Wolf!" he's crying.

Only once, in this ceiling. It's all he'll have time for.

Jake at 38

Sitting on the front steps of the trailer,
he hears the baby cry once,
but she falls back asleep and his wife doesn't wake.
It's early. He lights a Newport,
meditates on the menthol, squints at mosquitos
and blows smoke circles, watching them lift and
disappear over trailer and pines, dirt driveway and truck.

Crows laugh down sky and trees
on Jake, heavy with all
he's wrapped in—script writ
with wife and child, home and work.
Cool iron bars to grip and press his forehead against.

Jake sees the thought of himself, walking
separate and sure again, past a patch of fog.
This Jake stops as if surprised, locks eyes,
shakes his head. A much younger Jake.
More muscular and casually handsome.
With a warm toughness women wish to embrace
and a sinewy surety men hope to find in their mirrors.
Jake in a world he swore off,
thinking he wouldn't miss it. Until he did.
Mostly the women and possibilities.
The lack of ache. The delusion of invincibility.

Flicking the cigarette, he watches it
fizzle once in dew-jeweled grass.
The baby cries anew. The trailer shifts slightly
as his wife steps out of bed. She calls out,
"Jake? You there?"

On the Brooklyn-Queens Crosstown Local

Slouched in his seat, legs spread
like casual hunger, he stares down two girls
sitting across from him between Nassau and Greenpoint,
Greenpoint and 21st, 21st and forever.

Stiff baseball cap askew, white T-shirt extra long
and taut into white pants belted black at the roof of the pubic bone,
bare arms, muscle and shine, in the belligerent smooth
of youth. He's played lines in these cool shallows before.
Sisters or best friends with pretty red ribbons,
flags of sass and innocence, knotted in the brilliance of black hair.
Their gazes look down at unblemished shoes—ones
Mama bought Sunday, maybe, shoes that cannot
walk or run away, cannot find Papa to help
in the canned humanity of a subway. It's an unfamiliar strain
of fright, stilled by this jacklight of brown and white,
these awls called a man's eyes—eyes they do not meet
yet can't help but feel. Chance stranded them
across from impossibly low pants—as if in the brazen act
of being removed—across from his parted legs,
their playful purity an openly concealed grin,
cat mouth taking cat-joy in acts of mouse-misery.

Until finally the Court Square squeaking
of brakes. Until finally, he stands, height
wrapped in the impunity of youth, mid-aisle
till the doors open with their *wish* sound, till
he releases the bar, steps off, swaggers away,
not bothering to glance back once from the platform.
He has already forgotten these girls, these fish released
to water, gaping-grateful, regaining glint
and shine as they allow themselves a smile.

41

But it's brief, and the subway shivers and jerks forward, and the girls have no choice but to temper their breaths of freedom as they tunnel into the darkness ahead.

The Pursuit of Happiness

Once too busy for any mid-life crisis,
now embracing a late-life crisis,
his 60-something brain is like the kid pulled screaming
from the candy aisle of belief systems.

What is it he wants? What is it he lacks?
Online, articles about happiness swear
stress and dissatisfaction with one's body
only shorten shelf life.
But his body—bone, muscle, and skin
devolving and desiccating—sags and spots
brown like overripe fruit. Body in full-rebel bloom.
Body as traitor, as tag-along prison.

What is it he wants?
It starts with what he doesn't want.
Above ground or below.
Worms or dust.
Fire or ashes.

> *Eternal life?* asks that thorn called conscience. *Really?*
> *Admit it, coward. And be audacious. Add conditions.*

Very well, he says. Back to toned and unblemished.
The 20-year-old shell he remembers too well.
Through the sieve of memory,
where only good survives the straining.

> *I see. "If I knew then what I know now," and all that*
> *self-pity crap. How about rising from the dead? Hold on,*
> *though. Didn't Lazarus have to die twice, poor sod?*

What is it he wants? Let's start over, he says. Like shopping
genetically for baby: choosing where and when, color of skin,
eyes and chin. Screening movie renditions of himself
(auditioning bodies, faces, temperaments, *et* and joyful *cetera*).

> *You bored. You seeing I to I with the ennui*
> *hiding in eternity. Getting old, getting tense,*
> *needing reincarnation and other stimulants.*

WAVES OF WALDEN

"As far back as I can remember I have unconsciously referred to the experiences of a previous state of existence."
—Henry David Thoreau

Thoreau Knows

The mass of men lead lives of quiet desperation.

Making sense of things,
Trying to track

Nine pebbles of sadness
To their source.

Sly crows
Stole them a mile back,

But Thoreau knows
I should walk anyway

Under sun-coined trees
Thick with wood-thrush song

Till I reach undergrowth
Dense and itchy with the past

Till the air cools and I am near
Enough to con crow talk,

Mouths full, stories dark.

Saltmarsh Tanka

Slanting in the sun
birdhouse on a pole casts thin
watery shadows.
Cold and pale grass nest in a
box of fledgling November.

September Aubade

Wake up early, walk outside,
hear the shift of stars
that washed out yesterday's storm.

Catch the scent of Orion—
canvas leather and sweat,
his game bag
heavy with horizons.

Walk past houses, where
summer stipples the screens
of open windows.

Stop to listen:
      somewhere
      the sleep-slide of cricket song.
      Somewhere, possibility
      romancing hope
      while dawn gathers
      its fertile east.

Meditation Lesson

I can hear
peepers
in the beaver-flooded wood
the churn of water
under a frog's legs
the red fox kit's
high-pitched bark
two Great Horned Owls
hooing conjugal loneliness
too
the wind lifting
boughs of hemlock
ant legs crackling
over grass blades
the front doorknob twisting
the wood door cracking
thought's weight
pressing monkey branches
into its once well-
burnished broadside.

Breathe in…hold…
breathe out.

Breathe in…hold…
breathe out.

Old Dog Poem

Such a sweetness
in old dogs,

the way elbows
hard-knock the floor

as they lie heavily,
groan, and half-heartedly

scratch at sevens
stuck behind the years.

Getting close to the eyes
to glean old-dog thoughts,

you see two marble fogs,
orbed reflections

of a kitchen window
dimming behind you.

Her puppy kingdom at large.
Familiar, yet far.

Maine Deer Hunt

That Maine November wouldn't wait for winter.
Each morning I sat in a deer stand—simple slats hammered
between tree trunks—observing secret silences: me,
rifle, journal, pencil, thermos of coffee, and white breaths
rising to the dark loneliness of ravens wheeling overhead.

There was the moon's company, at least, snagged
and sagging pale against sharp black branches scraping sky.
A red squirrel visited, too, perching his pluck at a safe distance,
chattering so his tail shook in sharp squirrel syllables.

I heard ghost deer stepping through sticks and leaves
before the coffee lost its warmth. Then the toes,
despite boots and double socks. I took off my gloves,
opening to the blue lines of my coil notebook, scratching
12-point hopes until my fingers grew thick and red over cold
words and sentences leaning first Thoreau, then Hemingway.

On the third night, a nor'easter blew in. Before dawn, outside
the bedroom window, I heard wind and horizontal snow
while the others slept in. I got up to feed the Franklin stove
new wood and old *Bangor Daily News:* the smell and smoke
of paper and kindling, the crackle of fire building in confidence,
the airy rush of flue humming with heat. The orange glow
between stove cracks around the iron door, the way it coursed
new life into room and man. Such simplicity made me happy.

I brewed coffee to the broom-sweepy sounds of snow swiping
clapboards and sat on the brick foundation skirting the stove,
the back of my flannel shirt absorbing its radiance.
Then I opened a black Penguin Classics paperback: Turgenev's
Sketches from a Hunter's Album. It had a story, "Kasyan
from the Beautiful Lands," starting with the lines,

"I was returning from a hunting trip in a shaky little cart
and, under the oppressive effects of an overcast summer day's
stifling heat…I was dozing as I rocked to and fro."

Before long, words and fire lulled me like the hunter's coach.
Maybe it was the soft cast of the stove's hood lamp, the windows
whitening under a new day's antler-velvet winds, or the wood
burning in the Franklin's iron belly, but briefly, I felt like nothing
could touch me, like I might be foolish enough to live forever

while, outside, bedded in snow under heavy-limbed pine
and hemlock, ghost deer dreamed of Russian fields, of forests and
brooks, of plentiful berries and endlessly beautiful lands.

The Duck Blind

It's a long November walk
to the reservoir before dawn
under a horn moon and specks of white
dry and cold against the night.

Over the rows of frozen furrows
across a Connecticut cornfield's back:
razed stalks, torn roots,
hard clumps under heavy boots.

So pleasant the sky, dark and high,
as we gaze at our breaths' rise,
like thinning smoke, slow and dense,
lifting toward the stars' silence.

As we crest the hill, broken reflections
dance over the reservoir's surface:
silvery winks from the watery black
while cork ducks rattle in my canvas sack.

Boots, decoys, tinkling of retriever's tags—
life distilled to simplicities in three—till
the dog, anxious for the blind, begins to race
first far, then near, impatient with our pace.

The memory feels like only this morning: the itchy
cold of a fallen log permeating seats of pants,
the tender tendrils of thermos coffee's steam,
November morning waking from November dreams.

The tree line's black-scrim against the brightening east.
The cheerful cheep of chickadees flitting
from tree to bush to branch behind the blind.
Not thinking—just being—how it nourished the mind.

54

Dark Humor Tanka

Five black guillemots
legs stroking forward against
the outgoing tide—
fearless metaphors feathered
to their long journeys nowhere.

The Phoebe Nest

One April morning, just below the inner ledge
of a column, the slats of my porch broke out with
the white measles of bird shit. I had heard a mother
Phoebe's raspy fee-bee and, not wanting
the mess of daily excrement on my mahogany
or grass and mud crowning my column's crisply-
painted ledge, found two right-sized rocks near the road,
perching them there to thwart the bird's instincts.

As a child I loved visiting my uncle's farm
with its leaning barn of gray, splintering wood:
the way sun rays slanted through side windows, cracked
and dirty, showing motes of dust suspended in warm
and fragrant air. How the wooden doors on rusted rollers
remained open for swallows swooping in and out
in liquid arcs to nests propped on the lips of
lumber joists. Listening to the fecundity
of cheeping hatchlings' hunger and climbing
the hayloft once to see their small and comic old-man
heads, their fine sprouts of down and closed eyes.

Straws in beak, the mother Phoebe returns every morning
to the inner ledge of my porch, fluttering around the disorder
of my symmetrically-placed rocks. For a week she sang
from a nearby apple tree, maybe a song of confusion,
maybe of sadness or alarm, before flying into
the mouth of another spring day. I had no choice but to listen
first to the apple tree's silence, then the maples, oaks,
and pines and the pond they ringed, followed by Lyman Hill
looming behind, and finally the White Mountains whose
craggy caps scribed the western sky. Then I took
the rocks and threw their common sense into the woods.

A False Spring

After the long freeze,
winter cracks and
January rain eases
into its own fissures.

Water rakes
the west side's
cedar shakes
and, after hesitation,
gutter ice breaks,
releasing its birth flow
through downspouts:
the tin-thrum
of young tongues.

You never know
loneliness
till you hear
winter rain from
a new year's sky.

Riprap

Not a new puzzle poured over a card table,
     nor the symmetry of brick & mortar,
     but the disorder of last year's rocks
     reconstellated by the retreat of winter ice.

Each spring, stones in my hands,
     some uprooting lake-bottom mud clouds.

Each spring, silence stoned to sound
     as I lob large then medium then small
     building another riprap wall,
     scraping liver-colored leeches from my leg,
     watching tendrils of blood diffuse underwater.

Wearing nets of spider web as I move in & out,
     threading between bushes sharp with branches
     & soft with bee-hum thrum.

It's control marrying structure birthing order.
     It's the fine ache in my back,
     the kind rhythm in my bend & stand
     till I wade out to survey the land.

It's afternoon westerlies kicking up waves,
     darkening rocks
     to a harder-looking stoniness.

It's riprap gleaming, riprap breathing,
     riprap pretending permanence
     as earth & roots peek through the gaps,
     as shoreline meditates on loss,
     as waves sing soaked dirges
     to the sad, slow
     slip of the seasons.

Ticking

Before dawn, I wake
        to the bedside Big Ben

Listen for dark's
        dry drips

(Mechanical seconds,
        pennies of time)

Press clock
        to calibrated head

Fill the whorl of my ear
        with its countdown

Breathe bedroom air
        (cool, kind), think on

Inevitable ambushes
        (day, hour, second)

When exhale
        gives chase to inhale

Jumps and drags to a dust cloud
        the gazelle of my being.

Until friendly furniture and
        familiar walls softly sift to gray.

Until tick, tick, tick…light's
        dry drips herald another day.

The Pause Between

Only May but the wasps and yellow jackets are anxious
as October afternoons as their hum and buzz
bend toward the sweet rot of last year's garden.

Inside the ants scribe picaresques along the painted cracks
of old floorboards. Everything is leg life and antennae riddle.
Everything is secret restlessness and hidden destination.

One day the dragonflies appear sudden as the sun.
Speed and softness, they lash sky to air in silent seams.
One's barred wings and abdomen are pressing

to the warm dock slats. Another lights on the Chekhov book
you bought me, not realizing, like everything, it is a short
story too. Two fishermen sit in a boat across the lake—hunched

specks, tired voices carrying over the water, reminding me
of winter mornings, scrambled eggs in the iron skillet,
you coming up the hall in my flannel shirt. There's a north

wind off the back of the island and a noisy kingfisher on a dead
branch, each fashioning cold presence out of your absence.
A pine needle falls on my thigh. A loon looks across

the water, garnet-eyed and open-beaked. You said, after a loon
calls, it always waits for its mate to call back. You said
the pause between is the loveliest, loneliest hollow in the world.

Happy as a Clam Haibun

The gull peddles ankle-deep in shallow surf, foam-dancing, submerging its head to peck into sand. If it cannot yet grasp the shell, it dances anew: feet, beak, feet, beak. Then the pattern of patience unsands a crescent of clam and, mouth full, the bird takes to the sky over the tidal flats.

Until it feels the fall from a gull's beak
All the clam knows is the hardness of happy
And the darkness of delusion

Thoreau Reconsiders

In moments of despair,
Thoreau considered
the consolations of suicide

but there was no guarantee
that the other side would
offer the same grace of moonlight
against Walden's face,
or the wet smell of rotting leaves
plastered to roots and rocks
on Concord's paths,

or the nostrils' sense
for still-distant
snow—or the call of the
crow—or the west wind's song
in oak and maple tops,
or dawn's first scintilla
of sun dousing night's last
mourning star
of sadness.

Thoreau took comfort
in how none of these could
consider consolations
of other sides:

they were too busy
living on the only
side they knew.

OLD BEGINNINGS,
NEW BEGINNINGS

All the new thinking is about loss.
In this it resembles all the old thinking.
                                        —Robert Hass

My Old School

Time on my hands won't wash off.
I rub them hard: the grit of Boraxo powder,
The funk of metallic water in the boys' room
At the end of the gymnasium hallway.

Along the brick walls, brown radiators
Ping and clang as if newly started after
Holiday. I smell heat, dust, the stale
Odors of piss and locker room sweat.

The desks align perfectly in Miss Fisk's
Fourth-grade classroom. From the corner,
Our flag pledges allegiance to thirty-four
Students, scissors, glue, construction paper.

That fluorescent gleam on the floor tiles
And the Cortland on the teacher's desk,
The wax and skin—so bright and so crisp.
It must be the wiles of our janitor, Mr. Levesque,

But his cleaning closet is closed today and, last
Week, Dad claimed he saw him at the track,
Unshaven, cigar riding his lips, at the window,
Playing an exacta on If Only and Imagine That.

The Farmer in Time

Someone said her name was Sadie,
that it had been four summers since she died—
four summers her farmhouse
sat barren on Mayberry Hill, front
tagged by realtors, clapboards
chalked and grayed under successive Maine suns.
Last summer the house turned morose
like an old nun in dusty habit working her rosary,
counting beads, numbering the days.

This summer, though, upon my return,
daisies and goldenrod have bolted,
skirting the foundation. Rhode Island Reds
peck crabgrass out front; a pickup, split firewood
blanketing its bed, noses the open barn door.
Then the true sign: a sloped clothesline
tethering house to iron pole—shirts bellying
with wind, pant legs kicking sky
like drunken line dancers.

The south field, once lazy with wildflowers
and crickets, has been scratched to life, too.
A garden arches its back for the till.
Down-pricked tomato vines, heavy and newly-staked,
sniff for sun, buds and yellow star-blossoms
rich with the green pinch of life.

As I jog by, a young farmer
with a Deere baseball cap strides out the door,
solid in his plaid shirt and suspenders,
blue jeans and muck boots. He tilts his beard
west before walking into the mouth of the barn.
His wife, blonde-bunned, baby on hip,
opens the kitchen door and calls his name.

Caleb, I think. Caleb who will not hear
because his barn is storybooked with nesting swallows
and dry bales of hay and dust-beamed sunrays
slanting through cracked side windows. That is how
I like it, so I will not stop and say hello. Today or ever.
Like a Biblical drought or plague of locusts,
talk would destroy everything.

First-Person Solipsist

The end of the world?
Fire, the white coat scientists
will surmise. Detonations, radiation,
cloud totems rising with slow
impunity toward sleeping gods.

Or much gentler than that.
The redwing blackbirds' call
from wetlands outside my window.
The west wind whistling screens
dry after spring rain. The bedsheet
corner flipping onto my face.

Let's make it a blessing, then:
snow melt and scarlet epaulets.
The patois of March.
Checks and trills, lonely and secret
in their blackbird way, knowing the reason
this doctor's hand feels soft and warm
closing my eyes. The softness
showing his disdain for manual labor.
The warmth proving his body's ignorance
of just how close the end has come.

The last thing I will hear after such strange
intimacy is the nurse: "Dead?"
And the last thing I'll realize
is the harsher revelation: All of you are,
the moment March detonates and buries
my celebrity in sudden and steel,
obscuring what were once
earnest pupils on a world supposedly
without end, amen.

Rip

On seeing Confederate flags outside Maine households (2016-2020).

Maybe it was wrong, wishing I were Rip Van Winkle
so I could sleep four orange years away, wake, and shout,
This, too, has passed! to spontaneous dancing in the street.
But this folk tale fantasy was dismissed by a friend labeling
my silence a "moral cowardice." *And what if it didn't pass?*

Would you run to the Sleepy Hollow barbershop's pole of blue,
blood, and white; get the cynicism trimmed from your eyebrows;
have the indifference brushed from your beard? Would it be
too late by then? I asked, swiping sand motes from my eyes,
Q-Tipping lost opportunity from my ears.

Would I hear barking men, see boorish salutes, witness crisp
Stars and Bars flapping on flag poles along either side of
Main Street in this Free State of Maine, which buried
over 7,000 Union dead? *Yes,* he replied. *And return to another*
country entirely. One no amount of sleep could salvage.

When Russian Hackers Take Down the Grid

No doubt it will happen in winter. Dusk.
Brightness sucked by earth's thirst,
protest beeps from battery life supports,

code-reds blinking wild. You will think, a mere
blip, check the weather outside your window,
find 100% chance of night. You will think

to call, insistent and petulant, the utility company's
1-800. You may even wonder about accidents:
"Honda SUV (highly-rated by *Consumer Reports*)

Kneecaps Telephone Pole" (and damn it,
when will wires be exiled underground?).
If you are creative—and you will finally have time

to be—you will picture that car: steam hissing,
blue-green coolant bleeding and pooling,
fingering the pavement's fissured frost heaves.

Soon, air in the house will slip its hand over your shoulder,
tighten its grip on your clavicle. Cool will whisper "cold"
in the lacuna of your ear, elicit gooseflesh. Might as well

put your ear to the floor. Listen for hoofbeats
from the first rider's steed as romaine leaves relax
in the refrigerator, as rocky road ice cream warms

to the news in the freezer. Soon will come the sound of
the second horse, its rider phlegmatic and fanatical.
Russian ghosts in the machines will strike the flint

of your fear as you slip on sweater and coat, step outside
to the hooing of an owl, the drone of distant generators,
the moon shadow of your house spread dead against the lawn.

At the Midnight Hour

Going to Little Beach was Mark's idea.
We brought our flashlights to light-spear
sandy concrete beneath the boardwalk, to find
gritty quarters, dimes, prized Kennedy halves
newly-minted for the newly-dead. Two 12-year-olds,
we slipped coins into our pockets where they grew
warm and slippery, talismans against the night.

We'd never done it at midnight—walked barefoot
past the lichen-covered Indian grave on the forest floor's
brindled dark. The sand on the path cool and silky.
The ocean's black licorice split by a jagged boom
of moonlight. Breaking waves. The soft-sizzle
welcome our mothers warned us off of.

Reaching the spit of sand on the other side
of the wood, we saw the Sound, its milky scar again.
Then, 50 feet away, movement. Two people.
Clumps of clothes like small stone dogs
sitting at attention beside them. Woman and man
matted with sweat and sliding shadows.
We watched, shivering as forbidden found its fascination
in some ritual wrestling we'd never witnessed before.
The breaking waves. The quick, pitched cries.
Some spell salty and rhythmic.

"Holy shit," Mark whispered, but I was too busy breathing
the thick-aired wildness rolling in off the Sound.
When we heard a final, louder cry, it was like a bigger wave
catching us off guard. We seized our flashlights and ran,
sure it had signaled our discovery.

After that, everything blurred and burned.
Running and leaping. Spider webs and snapping sticks.
Back through wood and thicket scratching our arms.
Back where our faces turned tingly,
growing red and sticky with gossamers of guilt.

Love Poem for My Wife

After your birthday song,
our kitchen smells of the smoky years
and our kisses taste
of cream cheese frosting.

"This is nice," you say,
"but we don't really need
Valentine's Day or birthdays
to prove our love, do we?"
Questions like that are enough
to make time slacken with the sentiment,
days and calendar squares melt
into Jackson Pollock pools
of desire.

Then there's the way you sing
Sixties songs to the water's
background do-wops
against shower stall walls.
It calms me as I brush my teeth.
It makes me lose myself
in the embrace of your mirror steam.

And those evenings on the couch,
when you wonder if I might join you
to watch your *Pride and Prejudice*
DVD for the sixteenth time.

So serious yet naïve,
it makes me want to laugh,
collect your innocent smile and,
out of sheer selfishness, block
your view of Colin Firth forever.

Advice for Insomniacs

Sleep is a shifting school of fish
slippery with silver dreams:

off, on, out, in through the glistening hours,
leaving crenellated pillow treads

across my cheek. I find a sleep doctor and,
like any good American, expect solution

as pill: yellow, blue, round,
oblong—problem solved. But the doctor

doesn't prescribe so much as pontificate,
droning on until I begin to feel

warm and dozy, to grow nostalgic
for the snap of breeze-dried bed sheets

from my mother's backyard clothesline.
I think of bottling the spring-fed water

of her voice for a cool draught or two.
Then I can portage like Lewis and Clark

under hardwood and hemlock, cross
the Sacagawea-seen peaks, stop to curl

near a sun-diamond sea where the surf turns
rhythmical, where west winds lay washcloths

against the forehead, where sleep steals
into the restless conch of my being.

On Reading Frank O'Hara's *Lunch Poems* for the First Time

Who is this O'Hara typing so frankly, anyway? Engaging
in repartee with himself, playing words to the percussion
and sway of subway rumblings under his soles. Meals, walks,
living in the MoMA, dropping names like Lucky Strike butts—
poets, playwrights, artists, film makers, musicians, actors.
Et d'autres! The ease of Gallic words lacing their sleeves through
New York arms: *La joie de vivre* on 6th Avenue! *Le pain* on Park!
La moutarde on Madison!

This $1.25 paperback, so retro and sexy, so creased and shiny
from readers' oily finger whorls. So unrhymably orange, blue,
and white with its font City-Light. So damn James Dean: cigarettes
and fast cars, girls and open lips, windblown hair and line breaks
without a cause.

I ask the poet chewing pastrami and rye beside me, "What's
a Monogatari? Why Rachmaninoff's birthday? And do people
really fall in love with Lana Turner when she gets up?" His head
shakes in couplets as he incisors his sour pickle and flashes his
sauerkraut smile. At noon in the city, such questions invite sound
answers: delivery truck horns, *hum-colored cabs*, keytops
and typebars, *non* wooing *sequitur* till I feel like I'm conjuring
Camelot history from a 60s diner stool seat—red-vinyl squeak,
pedestal silver and sleek.

Imagine! Readers still mourning JFK and rhymes. Frost without
fedoras. Days when this *dejeuner* of ditties first slummed
the gum-quartered sidewalks of Gotham, *avante* and *garde*-ing
with Bazooka Joe pride, proper nouns tagging along like eager
little brothers: Koch and Ashbery. Verlaine. Crane. Rimbaud,
Dubuffet and *un autre* Frenchie named Reverdy. But most notably?
Lana Turner. Forever frozen. In some get-up or other.

Incroyable, these all new 55-year-old poems! I've chewed them
100 times over before swallowing (they'd be crunchier with
iceberg lettuce and more punctuation), but it's more the joy
of finding the long found. Like discovering America in 1592—
all in the land-ho of the beholder!

To a Depressed Friend

Sometimes, to make sure
You're still here,
Look up for cloud sustenance.

Be sure they are
Different from yesterday,
From an hour ago,

From when you were 15
And sky didn't matter
Because only pretty girls did.

Note how cumulus
Will be looking down
And naming what

Kind of human you're
Shaped like: mailman,
Archaeologist, student of rain.

On clear nights, rely on starlight.
Pentacles. Pulses.
Further proof of existence.

Rosa Raises Red Flags

I'm depressed, all right, my friend admits.
Always talking like I want to die

but acting like I'm worried about dying.
Convinced this fist-sized ache

is stage II stomach cancer,
sure my sharp back pains

point to an inflamed pancreas, worried
these migraines might be an astrocytoma

digging starry roots into
the fertile loam of my brain.

With logic like this in a world as
absurd as mine, you'd be depressed, too.

Rosa finally stops to smile, adding,
Isn't life sweet? Worshiping the god of irony?

I nod and allow it's so, fighting the salt-burn
of tears, watching her smile die its slow death.

Self-Diagnosis

The dog chewed the leather bookmark
you made me last Christmas.
I left it on the floor while reading that
book about diet and pain you bought,
as if all this can be laid at the feet
of nightshades or acidic foods or sugar in
the chocolate truffles and cherry scones you shouldn't
have bought from the bakery beside the bookstore.
So, if it seems like I'm making shit up to get out of
clipping hedges and weeding your lovely herb
garden, or of pulling apart the damn
drier with its new tumble-dry squeak,
or of power-washing the deck and staining
it with that natural tint you chose from the color wheel,
I'm not. As proof of my dedication
to diagnosis and my innocence in losing my place,
I can report that the word "myalgia"
means "muscular pain and tenderness,
especially when diffuse and nonspecific."
How's that for a fancy-ass term
in lieu of real answers?
So please forgive the dog his appetite.
It wasn't the book, at least. Just your tasty bookmark,
which must have looked to him like
a fine strip of beef jerky and tenderness.

Reading Bad Poetry on the Floor

Lying on the floor, I should continue reading
this book, but I'm distracted by a few bad poems,

thumbing back to acknowledgments,
wondering the how and the who and the why.

Soon the carpet around me affords
points of interest: The shotgun wedding of oatmeal

and wheat in its weave. The heat vent's nostalgic warmth.
The paisley curl echoing across a couch skirt.

Even the antique Singer sewing machine compels.
Embossed drawers and black iron hoops.

Leather belt. Treadle like hidden meanings.
Foot pedal still recalling the meter of Gram's pulse.

Practical imagery, true, so a nod to bad poetry is due.
It makes me notice, Buddha-like, more mundane poems

around me: the forced hot air, the pile density of Berber rugs,
the music in a drawer of miscellaneously beautiful buttons.

The Poetry of Naps

Not halfway through
this poetry book
and already somnolent

with stanzas, tenting
my eyes with a roof
shingled in verse,

my nose up its crevice
like a dog sniffing musk
and metaphor from its

dark divide. My face,
sheltered in the slant,
smells of paper and ink

spelunking for sleep
in that neat divot of night
where pages meet,

listening as my three
o'clock shadow and poetry
scratch against one another,

sandpaper inhales
and exhales until I'm rested,
until I'm ready to wake

to the rearranged letters
of poems rewritten under
dust jackets of darkness.

God's Hat Trick

After my scrubbed and gowned
body slipped from the MRI's womb,
the third rebirth from Siemens' tomb—
the hidden jackhammers, unanswered
door knocks, unheeded alarms—you ask
when I will hear back results.
"I don't know," I say. "I forgot to ask."

Driving our car, you mention
my phobia, unsure whether to leave it
alone. "A no-show," I reply. "They fit
a white mask over my face.
Like I was goalie for the Bruins, maybe."

To make you laugh because I need to hear it,
I add, "My big nose almost broke it, too. I closed
my eyes and dreamed it scraped low-lying clouds."

I don't admit this was no dream, or how close
these clouds—heavy as hammocks—sank
inside the antiseptic, concentric, claustrophobic hole-
iness downpouring its magnetic dissonance.

Or how I fought the din by feeding the machine
my past, summoning childhood in jumpy,
8 mm frames. I imagined the radiologists
analyzing results: grainy color shots of pratfalls
on Pee Wee hockey rinks and fumbled Statue of Liberty
plays on Pop Warner football fields. (October rain…
the smell of cigar smoke clouding bleachers…the damp
decay of dead leaves and mud in the end zones.)

"Was it a shutout at least?" you smile as we ride
back roads under Concord's hardwoods, sun and shade
swapping shadow and gold across my lap.

"Yes," pressing my head against the coolness
of the passenger side window, watching the open air.
"Like after the Zamboni. Nothing but ice, clean and white."

Praying for Miracles in a Time of Plague

Normal gets noticed
only once it's gone.
        Then it is a feeling
        fossilized,
        a yearning, a power lost
        in phantom limbs.

No one plans to
someday pray large
before a God
of Micromanagement—
        one who answers emails,
        returns phone calls,
        takes time to personally
        greet sufferers
        grasping purses and
        gripping hats in the
        Waiting Room of Death.

Yet here it is: pain
standing ramrod before
the Hollywood God of renown:
        White hair. White robe.
        White pity
        for egotists crying
        repeatedly,
        "Why me?"

For God will answer
as best He can.
Reach into His satchel.
Sow miracles
past their "best by" dates
in this earth
of His own creation—
           seven-day fields of drought,
           sun-stiffened soil, and shadows
           cast by vast
           cacophonies of crows.

MY BROTHER, MY SELF

"You only lose what you cling to."
—Guatama Buddha

Freudian Slip

In response to Freud and his obsession
with our obsessions, cultural anthropologist

Ernest Becker wrote, "Consciousness of
death is the primary repression, not sexuality."

My brother never had a chance because man's
primary phobia overtook him while he was

still reading up on Freud: exploring caves,
opening boxes, eating pears, and dreaming

under the influence of his own immortality.

Buddha's Rope

Buddha counseled the man
complaining of chronic pain:

Do not crave your past.
Mourning the body

of your youth unlocks the door
to the stranger you were,

making him stronger, more perfect
than he ever was, making you weaker,

more vulnerable than you'll ever be.
It's suicide to trust him now,

for the rope of the past
is woven with hemp and loss.

It will bind you—blister
skin until it burns—

distract you from the flint-
spark sunrise in pines' canopies,

the watery songs hiding in
orioles' breasts, the shoreline

smells of stone and grass,
mud and mint. Breaths rise and fall,

lungs ribbed by darkness yet
beautiful still: world in, world out,

birth's first scream,
death's last sigh. All part,

all whole, all sadness
and happiness letting go.

Moksha

It's nights when I'm feeling
stiff and old as
spaghetti sticking to itself

       in tepid water
       that I think of
       reincarnation and other stimulants

the lift in second winds
the buzz in repetition
the rush in do-overs

       where I get to remember
       and forget until some
       day-month-year

of yet another withering life
I finally enter
the rehab of nirvana

       forsaking reincarnation
       forever releasing
       the loyal rise of its circle

the lovely arc of its wheel
the familiar foreignness
of its forgiving circumference.

To Be

Caged in his aging body—the mortal slackening
of painful coil—the King of Denmark marks another decade.

There, Yorick's yellowed skull, maxilla and mandible mute
against a clump of bailey dirt. And here, the old king's ghost

coursing the ramparts, light and ethereal, the envy
of the Dane's stubborn flesh. For despite age

and to spite disease, the body fights to stay alive
through Act V (after any grand *exeunts,* before any

hey nonny, nonnies). Alas, Hamlet! Time fastens like a tick,
fat and gray with the years. Walking the cold flagstones

of senescence, strapped in stockings smoothing
varicose veins, intoxicated by soliloquys staring back

from cups of rheumy reflection, he wakes
each morning simply *to be* as he wrestles eternity.

My Brother's Thirteenth Halloween

That was the year our neighbor, Cherie, came over
and popped red wax lips into her mouth. Chastely
she kissed you with them, bro, not knowing that time would
leave its lipstick on your cheek. This was when death
was a plaything, an end-of-October thing. The R.I.P.
headstones Mom bought for the front lawn. The dancing
skeletons, joints jumpy with a string that lent us control.
The black-caped possibilities of being pretend dead.
Pale cuspids. Pulsing necks. Silver thrills from passing
mirrors and only seeing couch and lamps look back.
Remember? You and me alive as a team, bro?
Still young under the masks, still invincible, still in a place
where nothing could touch us, not even the approaching
Day of the Dead, not even the nights I'd travel to get there?

Cain-ish, Abel-ish

Brothers by blood,
one long after, one long before.
                    Cain criminally lonely,
plagued by pain, sickness, bolts of wrinkling.
Hostage in a body, doing time
behind his bars of bone. The atrophy
of muscles, the numbness of neuropathy,
the ache of time's joints.

And you, Abel. Lying in the casket of conscience,
your smile a curling Polaroid magneted
to the garage fridge door.
Abel, who carried the Summer of Love
forward six short years. Unfettered by pride.
Free of jealousy. Man-boy inoculated from change:
wheat sheaves of hair, lazy ropes of muscle,
two facet-blue irises and 32 teeth, strong and firm.
                    Abel unsilenced by the unseen
years, slamming memory's door as he enters
Cain's mind from outside, the smell of wind
and woodsmoke riding his flannel shirt.
Abel and laughter caroming off the wall of years.

Uselessly, Cain flees to the garden hip-high with weeds.
The tree that begat a stump.
The serpent that begat a death.
Months pass like the slow indignities,
years like the rusty knife of remorse,
                    because dying of time is a difficult business,
while staying young forever is easy
once the deed is done.

Act V

Once they put the die in his diagnosis,
life becomes a misnomer, five stages he doesn't
want to heed, even though psychologists have the
need to name, quantify, and order such matters.

Stages are useless once the chaos of limits
is turned loose. He has come to trust
only the creaky stage he's stepped on blindly,
the one where he stares into a dark audience

of hidden months and numbers, each as
indifferent as the next. One where suddenly
looking at Orion's belt or listening to wind blow
through pine trees is enough to make a man cry.

Another Hereafter

It's cold as crow-call here as I wake
from the last dream of self.

The past, lonely and hungry, seeks the tenderness
that fed it. Like windblown leaves, dead

memories catch at the fence of former
beings: orange then gray embers in the wood

stove, a train horn in the night, the waxy odor
of a tin of crayons. Or the candy lip gloss-taste

from a kiss, the false warmth of a cigarette,
the burn of whiskey-breakfast hairs of the dog.

The patience of pain that collects life's debts
and, upon arrival, politely declines departure.

Doctors. Specialists. Diagnoses. White flags
called pain medicine. Hospice smells, hearing

gathered loved ones' small talk, dimmed lights.
Last room behind a last door on a last day.

And here, now, like a child again, head facing
up, craving help to navigate the crossing, forced

to hear history's plow, its steel scraping New England
soil, stones, shards of buried glass. Desperate

to breathe blue and sweat sky again. If only
one had placed *The Book of the Dead* beside me.

I could reach down to grasp its grit and wisdom
in the vice of my hands. I could lift its 49 days

to my face. I could translate through the coin
of closed eyes and finally turn the page.

The Body Fights to Stay Alive

against the brain's better judgment,
but the brain follows in the dance of life,
the body leading like Fred Astaire,

so let's say we fox trot toward that corner
there, far from this depression thing (playing violin)
and that death thing (beating the drums)
by stimulating a drug called memory

because memory comma long-term goes blessedly
deep in the brain—wiser and simpler in its formative,
cauliflower days when it did not think so much because
it was too busy blindly following the body.
You know, like that boy without free will flying off the end
of Winslow Homer's whip on the playground of his
one-room schoolhouse (and oh, but to call recess on pain!).

Back then the body comma sensual was busy discovering
itself ("Hand, ho!" from the crow's nest of curiosity),
wondering important things like whether someone named Kathy
would discover it, too, by supplanting its sovereign flag
with her own coat of arms (and hands and mouth
and what do we have *here*?)

On cue comes Therapist Susan, interrupting again: "Really,
I had in mind more innocent topics."

You mean, like waking up and barefooting
into that darkest-before-dawn kitchen to the waiting love
of those pilot flames, those cozy teardrops of blue under the hood
of our gas stove? Or the time I found Bicycle cards
from Mom and Dad's Michigan Rummy party
and slid two Jokers into the toaster (going down!),
browning them till their conical bells smoke-jingled alarm.

One eventually cried (in Middle English, methinks), "Uncle!
Uncle!" and the other laughed, "Fire, dammit!" until I unplugged
the toaster and shook their singed motleys free for fear
their shouts would wake my parents (who were sleeping their
Michigan Rummy and Cokes off).

"When life gets rough" (read: is shadowy from the Valley
of Death), Susan interrupts, "keep taking trips to more pleasant
experiences, moments of less tension. Maybe your firsts, where
the joy was real. Iconic moments like the first kiss or your first car
or happy memories when your brother was alive or a memorable
Christmas." (Couched Mental Note: Christmas. Always
Christmas—what psychologists call the Comfort Food of Recall.)

Susan doesn't realize how impressionable
a brain (follower!) I have. She doesn't know that the first kiss
happened to be Clara C., of all girls, at a 7th grade party playing
spin the bottle with an empty 7-Up. A 7-Up neck that picked
Clara (why not Kathy?). Briefly exciting,
true, but the kiss was a first for her, too, because her little tongue,
small and stiff as a stoned snail, darted its pink head
in and out of my mouth, bringing with it the gold patina
of Doritos and Schlitz, and no, I cannot erase that memory
from my mind, and yes, it set me back four Kathy months
while I repeated to myself (because I didn't much *think* then,
as you'll recall), "Really? This is it? Like a fleshy
cuckoo-bird clocking my mouth 12 times over?"

Speak, memory, of the cold grip on that Dodge Dart
steering wheel turning February's corner on our street,
of the black ice-glide of bald Firestones, of the green-lit dashboard,
of the short-on-warmth, long-on-radio static car cave,
how it still smelled of Uncle Henry's (he gifted it as a tax write-

off) Winstons, the ashtray jammed shut with bent butts,
the filters sticking out as if shot in the act of escaping, the ribboned
red ones reflecting the creases of Aunt Harriet's lipstick.

And, to make you feel happy and confident under that framed
certificate of license, Susan, let me create
a Christmas morning when my long-gone brother and I
did *not* use my parents' bed as a trampoline
while rhythmically chanting, "Wake up! Wake up!
Santa came!" like other kids.

Oh, no. We plugged in the tree lights
in the living room's 4 a.m. holly-holy so our eyes could
gather the glitter of gift boxes and wrapping paper and virgin bows
under the electric red-yellow-green graffiti of bubble lights
that gulped as if repeating the Eve's gingerbread excesses.
We'd purposely almost-clench our eyes, Susan, so that
our eyelashes gave the gift of gorgeous, gauzy effects,
expanding, shrinking, sending us into Santa swoons
as if drugged by his materialistic manna, as if a festive magician,
maybe, had taken our wishes, conjured Christmas rabbits,
and multiplied the gifts with a swoop of his Peter Rabbit wand.
All that abracadabra wizardry by me and my brother, who
not only stayed young but is getting younger by the Christmas.

Can I stay there for good, Susan? In the past with him, I mean?
Because the present is kind of crowding me, and your familiar,
friendly voice is getting ready to say *time* again, I know it—
my time is almost up.

How the Dead Speak

I wondered, but my brother claimed no,
it's never the dead speaking all at once
when aspen leaves scratch shivery
dialects against midnight's window.

Same for ocean surf, he said,
when waves of foam and foment
break out in sizzle and doubt.

The dead don't speak individually, either,
he insisted, so forget that fat June bug ping
on summer's window screen
and any wisdom gleaned.
Hard-wrought words like that
are dismissed by the living, he assured me.
Mere bluebottle buzz, they'll say,
or bumble bee drunk on blooming day.

More likely than any of this? As my brother
not only predicted but eventually proved himself,
the dead speak not at all. Winds fall.
Seas flatten. The night peers back.

Coda: Miss Emily Speaks

"But it is growing damp
and I must go in,"
Emily Dickinson wrote
to a friend near the end.
"Memory's fog is rising."

It dissipates
into bottomless night
and the thirsty hollow
of the moon's borrowed light.

It leaves a canvas
of earth and amnesia,
a *tabula rasa*
where revelation
bends back toward its genesis,
dying to say (again and again),

"In the beginning…"

*

About the Author

Ken Craft, who grew up in Connecticut and now lives in Maine, is the author of *The Indifferent World* (FutureCycle Press, 2016) and *Lost Sherpa of Happiness* (Kelsay Books, 2018). His poems have appeared in *The Writer's Almanac, South Florida Poetry Journal, Pedestal Magazine, Spillway*, and elsewhere. You can visit him at kencraftauthor.com.

www.ingramcontent.com/pod-product-compliance
Lightning Source LLC
Chambersburg PA
CBHW022013080426
42733CB00007B/580